A CHILDHOOD IN TIBET

A Childhood in
TIBET

Tendöl's Story

THÉRÈSE OBRECHT HODLER

PENGUIN
VIKING
An imprint of Penguin Random House

VIKING

USA | Canada | UK | Ireland | Australia
New Zealand | India | South Africa | China

Viking is part of the Penguin Random House group of companies
whose addresses can be found at global.penguinrandomhouse.com

Published by Penguin Random House India Pvt. Ltd
No: 04-010 to 04-012, 4th Floor, Capital Tower -1,
M G Road, Gurugram -122002, Haryana, India

Penguin
Random House
India

First published in Switzerland 2019
First published in Viking by Penguin Random House India 2021

Copyright © Thérèse Obrecht Hodler 2021

10 9 8 7 6 5 4 3 2 1

The views and opinions expressed in this book are the author's own and the
facts are as reported by her which have been verified to the extent possible,
and the publishers are not in any way liable for the same.

ISBN 9780670094202

Typeset in EB Garamond by Manipal Technologies Limited, Manipal
Printed at Thomson Press India Ltd, New Delhi

www.penguin.co.in

Contents

CONTENTS

Foreword

Tibet is an ancient land whose people have a long history, and a rich culture deeply rooted in Buddhism. In the 8th century, a Tibetan King, Trisong Deutsen, invited the Indian master Shantarakshita from the historical Nalanda University to establish Buddhism in the Land of Snow. The Nalanda tradition placed special emphasis on the study of logic and philosophy, an approach preserved today in the Tibetan Buddhist tradition.

Following Communist Chinese invasion of Tibet, terrible atrocities occurred in the east and northeast of Tibet resulting in the destruction of villages and monasteries in response to resistance by people from these regions against Communist Chinese subjugation. Thousands of Tibetans, spiritual teachers and other leaders among them, were humiliated, imprisoned, tortured and even killed. Refugees arriving in Lhasa from these areas corroborated the sad and horrific events.

Despite our sincere efforts at peaceful co-existence, Chinese authorities in Lhasa were intent in crushing any form of resistance. As a result, these events led to the Tibetan People's Uprising of 1959.

It is now over 60 years since a large number of Tibetans, including myself, were forced to flee Tibet. The generation of Tibetans who lived through this critical period is fast dwindling. It is therefore important to preserve memories of a freer Tibet while there are still people who can relate their first-hand perspective on this important moment in global history.

"A Childhood in Tibet" on Tendol Namling is the story of the life of a Tibetan family and a child born at this sad point in Tibetan history. Tendol is the youngest daughter of the late Paljor Jigme Namseling, then one of Tibet's four *Tsipons*, or Finance Secretaries. She spent the first 22 years of her life under Chinese rule. The book not only conveys the story of her life in Tibet but also the unflinching determination of fellow Tibetans to preserve our rich Tibetan Buddhist culture. It provides us with a glimpse of the changes in Tibetan society, brought about by Communist China's assault on Tibet's identity, religion, culture of peace and compassion. It also highlights the resilience of the Tibetan people as they work to sustain their distinctive culture. It is, at its core, a testimony to the Tibetan people's peaceful struggle for freedom.

I hope this book will help readers to understand better not only the tragedy that has befallen Tibetans, but also the significance of our peaceful aspiration for freedom and dignity, an aspiration that can speak to people in every culture and situation.

14 February 2020

Author's Note

In March 2019 Tendöl Namling turned sixty. Just as old as the Tibetan uprising. She was born on the same day the Dalai Lama escaped Lhasa under the cover of darkness, disguised, when the People's Liberation Army (PLA) of China ruthlessly suppressed the uprising of his people. She spent the first twenty-two years of her life under the Chinese rule. As the daughter of a high-ranking Tibetan government official, she experienced the brutality of China's 're-education' policy with full force. She has many painful memories of those years and a few crumpled photos which she always carried with her. The photos with her friends and cousins in Lhasa, smiling as if nothing had happened. Whenever the girls saved some money they posed for portraits in Chinese photo studios.

Tendöl, like thousands of other Tibetan (and also Chinese) youths, worked for years on road construction. She hid the photos under her pillow and cried herself to sleep at night. She did not possess any documents from this tragic period except the arrest warrant for her mother, who was sentenced to ten years in prison. As I was researching for this book, Tendöl often had difficulty giving me accurate information. When exactly was she doing road construction? When was she allowed to go to school for a short time? When did she complete her apprenticeship as a motor mechanic?

But she clearly remembered her feelings of those years. The anguish that her mother might be executed, the longing for her caring love. The aggravating hunger that drove her to eat pig-food in a Chinese garrison. The horror of the public executions that she was forced to attend. The corpses in the courtyards of the prisons. The defencelessness against men in uniform.

Tendöl wanted her painful childhood to be recorded so that the history of Tibet, and the repression by China that continues to this day, will not be forgotten. Her memories were buried deep in her innermost being and came back in bits and pieces, often out of context. Sometimes, she wiped away a tear from her eyes, especially when talking about her mother. But mostly, she told the story of her childhood as if she were talking about another person in another world.

Although she was not allowed to practise her faith under the Chinese rule, she embraced the Buddhist principles from an early age; she believed that things come and go, that nothing is permanent. She was able to let go and never lost faith in the positive path. This belief saved her during her childhood in Tibet and was always with her in Switzerland.

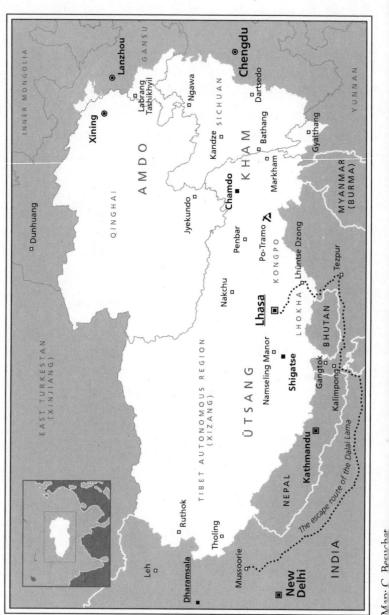

Map: C. Rescher

The summer palace of the Dalai Lamas in Lhasa recording the official ceremony when the Tibetan Government requested His Holiness the 14th Dalai Lama become the Political Leader of Tibet on 17 November 1950. Mural painted by Amdo Jampa 1955-56.

Encircled on the mural is Tendöl's father.

March 1959. An Uprising and a Birth

On 17 March 1959, the twenty-four-year-old Dalai Lama escaped Lhasa disguised as a soldier as night falls. Undetected, with a few loyal companions, he marched past the huge crowd of Tibetans that gathered to protect their leader with their lives. The fate of Tibet then changed forever. A week earlier, on 10 March, the Chinese military commander invited His Holiness the Dalai Lama to the army headquarters, but without his bodyguards. The Tibetan uprising broke out. The fear that their leader could fall into the hands of the occupying People's Liberation Army was

Around 30,000 Tibetans gather under the walls of the Potala to protect the Dalai Lama with life and limb. The Tibetan uprising breaks out on 10 March 1959.

unbearable for the Tibetans. They erected barricades in the narrow streets of Lhasa while the PLA positions artillery in the city. Leaflets called for resistance against the Chinese invaders. Rumours of treason and kidnapping made the rounds. Nomads passing through Lhasa whispered of tens of thousands of Chinese soldiers being in position at the boundaries of the city.

In his summer residence, the Norbulingka, the Dalai Lama discussed the critical situation with his advisors. If he stays, there will be violence. If he leaves, there will be violence as well. Two days later, on 19 March, when the word of the Dalai Lama's escape became public in Lhasa, street fighting between Tibetans and Chinese soldiers broke out. Poorly armed Tibetans faced overpowering Chinese military might. The PLA stationed in Lhasa since 1951, brutally crushed the uprising. 'The Tibetan problems must be solved by force', telegraphed Chairman Mao Zedong. Tens of thousands of Tibetans died in the following days in hand-to-hand battles and under artillery fire. Lhasa's three main monasteries, Sera, Ganden and Drepung, were destroyed, thousands of monks were arrested or executed, their monasteries destroyed and irreplaceable Buddhist scriptures burnt. After a few days, the Tibetan resistance was shattered.

Exhausted, the Dalai Lama and his companions arrived in India on 31 March. The adventurous escape, often at night, on foot or on horseback, in a small yak-leather boat across the Kyi Chu River (Brahmaputra) and in a snow flurry over the Sabo-La Pass, turned out to be successful. Still on Tibetan soil, the Dalai Lama revoked the infamous '17-Point Agreement' of 1951, which Tibetan officials were forced to sign by the People's Republic of China. The Indian prime minister, Jawaharlal Nehru, allocated available land to the Tibetans in the foothills of the Himalayas. The Dalai Lama was permitted–as the spiritual, but not

The Dalai Lama (on a white horse) on the escape journey. In Lhokha, Paljor Jigme Namseling meets the Dalai Lama and the entourage. His Holiness gives him a bead from his prayer rosary in recognition of his service to Tibet. Tendöl still wears it every day. © OHHDL

political head–to lead a Central Tibetan Administration in Dharamsala, but (officially) not a government in exile. Over the next few years, tens of thousands of Tibetans followed the Dalai Lama into exile and continued to regard him as their political leader as well.

In the midst of these tragic events, little Tenzin Dolma, called Tendöl, was born in Lhasa under dramatic circumstances as the last child of the Namseling family. Choekyi was in labour when Chinese armed officers came to arrest Tendöl's mother, the wife of Tibet's secretary of

Tenzin Gyatso, the Fourteenth Dalai Lama, at Birla House, Mussoorie (India) after the successful escape from Tibet. © Getty Images

state for finance. They lifted the blanket, saw blood and left the mother alone at the time. But, shortly after Tendöl's birth, a friend assisting Choekyi as midwife was arrested in place of the mother.

It was not in Tendöl's fate to meet her father, Paljor Jigme Namseling, who joined the Tibetan Khampa resistance and eventually escaped to India. A pain that she carries with her all her life. As *butruk*, a child of class enemies, Tendöl, pays a high price for her origins. Her father, a high-ranking Tibetan civil servant and member of the upper classes, owner of Namseling Manor, a seventeenth century property on the banks of the Kyi Chu, embodies for the communist invaders the Tibetan feudal society which was to be exterminated.

Eighteen Months Earlier

In September 1957, Tendöl's mother, Choekyi, her five children, Soyang, Dolkar, Tenzing, Tenor and Ngodup–as well as their cousin Pema and half-sister Sodon–had travelled to India under the ploy of going on pilgrimage. With an entourage of horses and pack animals, loaded with plenty of supplies for the long and arduous journey, the family and two companions crossed the Nathu-La Pass on foot, the border between Tibet and Sikkim, 4300 metres above sea level. Nobody imagined then that this pass would be closed and the border to Tibet sealed off for decades until today. Choekyi knew that this time around they were not real pilgrims like a year earlier, when she and the children had travelled

United in a garden at Kalimpong: Soyang, Dolkar, Tenor, Ngodup, Choekyi, Tenzing (from left).

to Bodhgaya, the place of the Buddha's enlightenment in India. This trip was about bringing their eldest daughters to safety. Since the invasion of the PLA forces in the early fifties, the pressure on Tibetans had increased rapidly. The Chinese tried by, all means, to lure as many Tibetan children as possible into Chinese schools. Many upper-class Tibetans, including the Namseling family, wanted to prevent their children from being raised in a communist system and sent them to missionary schools abroad. So Choekyi brought her three older daughters to Kalimpong in India and enrolled the girls in the Catholic St. Joseph's Convent.

Choekyi spent five months in Kalimpong. The twenty-eight-year-old enjoyed the colourful flora, the mild climate and especially the last days she was able to spend with all her children together. She accompanied the girls to the cinema, they listened to music, sang and danced. Then Choekyi returned to Lhasa with her two youngest, Tenor and Ngodup, and with a heavy heart leaving Soyang, Dolkar and Tenzing back in India.

On their way back to Tibet, they met a large number of Tibetans fleeing to India. Choekyi became increasingly apprehensive not only with regard to the situation in Lhasa but also to the future of Tibet and of her own family.

Choekyi (left) with her niece Pema in Kalimpong.

The three sisters of Longchoe Khangser from Shigatse: Tendöl's mother Choekyi (right) is the youngest. Kaldon Lungsher (centre) was married to an aristocrat, became a nun and now lives in Lhasa at the age of 92. The eldest, Pema's mother, Yangchen Dolkar (left), took in Choekyi's youngest children when her sister was arrested. She became a nun and died in Dharamsala at the age of 71.

China's Seizure of Power Tears the Family Apart

The Namseling family have been in Tibetan public service since the reign of the Fifth Dalai Lama. Tendöl's great-grandfather, a general, was killed in 1904 when the British-Indian army invaded Tibet. Her father, Paljor Jigme Namseling, began his Tibetan government service in 1925; from 1935 he spent four years as a military commander on the eastern border between Tibet and Xining; in 1940 he became governor of Shigatse, the second largest city in Tibet. Twice-widowed, and already the father of three daughters, he met Choekyi, who was twenty years younger

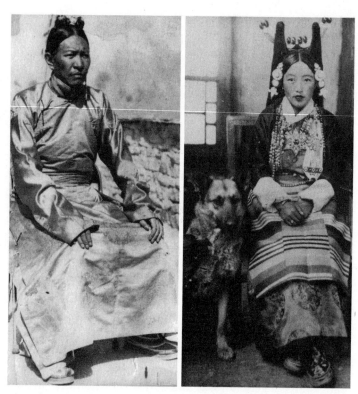

As governor of Shigatse, Paljor Jigme Namseling, Tendöl's father, meets
the twenty-years-younger Choekyi who immediately falls in love with the
'tall, strong, incredibly beautiful man' and 'cannot turn her eyes from him'.
They marry in 1944. Their marriage is very happy for 15 years, until the
political events separate the couple forever.

than him. They married in 1944 and two years later they moved to Lhasa, where Paljor Jigme became one of four state secretaries in the Ministry of Finance.

Paljor Jigme and Choekyi Namseling lived in a two-storey house in Khado Labrang, in the centre of Lhasa. The house was given to their son Tenor, the sixth Khado Rinpoche. It had a courtyard surrounded by small buildings and rooms. A family they befriended from the Kham region also lived there. Paljor Jigme rode daily on horseback to work at the Potala. The children had deep respect for him and entered his room only with his explicit permission. Tendöl's older sister, Dolkar, has happy memories of those days. She attended an ordinary school with her siblings and lived a seemingly normal childhood. When she was about seven-years-old, however, more and more Chinese appeared in Lhasa. The children didn't understand what was going on in their homeland but noticed that their life was about to change and that their parents were deeply worried.

They could feel how much the political situation weighed down their father. After the Chinese invasion of eastern Tibet in 1950, many Khampas fled their region and settled in Lhasa. A frequent guest at the Namseling house was the legendary Andrugtsang Gonpo Tashi, who had founded the Khampa resistance force, Chushi Gangdruk (which Namseling would join in 1958). Long discussions frequently took place behind closed doors. Choekyi

Choekyi and Paljor Jigme with little Tenor in their garden in Lhasa.

brought tea to the men. Except for her, no outsiders were allowed to enter the room or to know who was taking part in the conversations.

Since the beginning of the 1950s, the political situation in Tibet, and especially in Lhasa, was extremely tense. In addition to the fundamental dissatisfaction, the food supply in Lhasa and the surrounding regions deteriorated massively due to the presence of an overwhelming number of Chinese troops. At that time Tendöl's father belonged to a secret group of high-ranking government officials and merchants from the east of Tibet who had set themselves the

The parents Namseling with their only son, the Sixth Khado Rinpoche.

goal of fighting the Chinese occupation by all means.[1] Its members were well connected with the existing resistance outside the capital. The Tibetan People's Association founded in Lhasa addressed a petition to the Chinese occupiers in 1952. Paljor Jigme presumably played a major part in drafting this document. It listed six points for the 'improvement of relations between the Chinese and the Tibetans'. The tone of the petition was diplomatic, but the demands were clear; according to this document, on one

---

[1] Melvyn C. Goldstein, *A History of Modern Tibet*, 2007, vol. 2, p. 328-340; Tsepon W.D. Shakabpa, *A Political History*, 1984, p. 305

hand, social reforms should be carried out by the Tibetans themselves and, on the other hand, the role of Buddhism and the Dalai Lama as head of the Tibetans should be maintained and the survival of the monasteries guaranteed. In addition, Chinese troops were to be withdrawn and Tibet was to retain the prerogative of the economy, trade and national defence. In particular, the export of Tibetan wool and ingredients for traditional medicine should be allowed again. Under these conditions, Tibet would have become a kind of a Chinese protectorate, but would have retained its own government and institutions. This petition has never been implemented, just as all subsequent Tibetan attempts to engage in dialogue have been rejected by Beijing.

Paljor Jigme, like most Tibetans, mistrusted the '17-Point Agreement for the Peaceful Liberation of Tibet', which the Tibetan government was forced to sign in Beijing in 1951 which also brought about the Chinese annexation of Tibet. This agreement was revoked by the Dalai Lama in 1959 as a treaty signed under duress.

Dolkar, who arrived as an eleven-year-old student at the Pestalozzi Village in Trogen, Switzerland, with her sister Tenzing, carefully kept all of her father's letters. He wrote about the political system of Tibet and held the opinion that the rule by clergy and the nobility, as well as the theocratic structures, had not always been in the best interest of the

Paljor Jigme Namseling (far right) with three members of the Tibetan Ministry of Finance.

people. He clearly committed himself to reforms and more social justice.

In mid-October 1958, under pressure from the Chinese, Namseling was asked to lead a delegation to negotiate the disarmament of the Chushi Gangdruk resistance force, whose approximately 8,000 fighters faced 40,000 PLA soldiers. He travelled to Lhokha in southern Tibet and handed over the message from Lhasa to the leaders of the resistance. Instead of bringing about the dissolution of the group, he joined the resistance–to the surprise of the Chinese generals. Less than a year later, the Tibetan resistance was

Choekyi and her son, Tenor Khado. In mid-October 1958, when her husband, Paljor Jigme, is sent on a mission to disarm the Chushi Gangdruk resistance force in southern Tibet, Choekyi, three months pregnant with Tendöl, is filled with apprehension that 'if anything went wrong, this could be our last farewell', which indeed it proved to be.

overwhelmed and Paljor Namseling fled to India, at the risk of his life. At that time, he did not yet know that his youngest daughter, Tendöl, had been born in Lhasa. He never met Tendöl and never saw his wife, Choekyi, again.

In March 1959, the Namseling girls in Kalimpong listened on the radio to the news of the uprising of Tibetans and the brutal clampdown–but they had no idea what had happened to their parents. They no longer received remittances to pay their school fees and began to sell their Tibetan coral and turquoise necklaces. Neither did they know about the birth of their youngest sister, Tendöl, nor that their father had joined the Tibetan resistance and fled to India.

In May 1959, Paljor Jigme Namseling finally arrived at his daughters' home in Kalimpong. The ten-year-old Dolkar was struck by[2] the sight of her father, exhausted and emaciated, the expression of overwhelming sorrow on his face. He was a broken man. His emotion and grief afflicted Dolkar. He told the story of the tragic events in Tibet. He could not understand the cruel and destructive fury of the Chinese. He mourned friends and relatives who had died. The biggest pain, however, was the sorrow for his own family left behind in Lhasa. Choekyi, his young

---

[2] Herzsprung, A Tibetan story from Pestalozzi Children's Village, Eva Sieber, p. 7 – 13, Typotron Issue 23, 2005.

wife, little Ngodup and the only son, Tenor. And the sixth child that Choekyi had given birth to in the meantime. The borders to Tibet were sealed off, but Paljor Jigme had learned of the birth of Tendöl, his youngest daughter. Soon he received a picture of Choekyi with the three little ones, which had been smuggled out of Lhasa and secretly brought to Kalimpong. But the four family members in Tibet were now living at the mercy of the Chinese occupiers. Paljor Jigme had no means to help or protect them. This powerlessness, and the uncertainty about the fate of his wife and three children remained with Paljor until his death in 1973.

This picture was taken for her father after Tendöl's birth and smuggled to Kalimpong.

Re-education of the Class Enemies

In 1957, Mao Zedong introduced the system of 're-education through work' in China[3]. Two years later, the Chinese relentlessly began re-educating the Tibetans. First and foremost, this affected the Tibetan upper class. Between 1960 and 1962 the so-called social reform was directed against them, the class enemies. All those who had previously worked for the Tibetan government, the ruling

---

[3] In 2013 Beijing abolished the system of re-education through work (*laojiao*). Hundreds of labour camps were closed in China. But since 2017, new re-education and indoctrination camps were opened in the north-western province of Xinjiang. Over one million Muslim Uyghurs and other ethnic minorities have been incarcerated.

families, large landowners, lamas, members of monasteries and the military, merchants, artists, scholars and all their family members were divided into different 'classes'. Their children were branded as butruk, occasionally insulted by other Tibetans, pelted with stones and sent to road construction camps instead of going to school.

The artificial lake fronting the Potala at the centre of Lhasa was created by the forced labour of the butruk. Even today it is considered by Tibetans as a memorial to the suffering of the children.

'Re-education' also involved the confiscation of all private possessions, every single object belonging to a Tibetan. Most of them lost all that they owned. From then on, people lived in a 'nobody-house', and 'nobody' would take care of its maintenance. For the time being, Choekyi was lucky. Her big house in Lhasa had been confiscated, but with her three children and her grandmother she found shelter in her sister Yangchen Dolkar's[4] house. Yangchen was also the mother of Tendöl's cousins Pema (who already stayed in Kalimpong at that time), Lochoe and Rigzen.

---

[4] Yangchen Dolkar was married to a merchant from Kham named Dhoyontsang who had participated in the uprising of 1959 against the Chinese occupation. He was arrested and imprisoned in a Chinese labour camp. He starved to death alongside seventeen of twenty Tibetans imprisoned with him.

They considered themselves lucky that, unlike many other Tibetan families, they were allowed to stay together.

The spacious house of Tendöl's aunt had a courtyard with small rooms surrounding it. In the past, the aunt had rented out three rooms. Now twelve families were already accommodated in her home. Each family was assigned a room. Choekyi and her three children also had a room. All inhabitants of the house had an identity card, on which the names of the flatmates were entered. It was not unusual for Chinese officials to show up in the middle of the night to carry out checks. If someone was absent, or if an extra person was counted, all residents of the house had to admit their guilt the next day in a so-called 'struggle session'– *thamzing*–and face accusations and beatings.

In addition to the 're-education of class-enemies', the Chinese Cultural Revolution creates havoc in Tibet from 1966-1976. (Forbidden Memories, Tsering Woeser). © Woeser

Thamzing

For the population, these struggle sessions were worse than death or torture, says Tendöl. They took place every evening after work and lasted until midnight. The Tibetans were forced to criticize and beat each other, hurt and humiliate each other both physically and mentally. Children had to testify against other children or against their parents, neighbours against neighbours, pupils against pupils, tenants against landowners, former servants against their landlords. Children had to spit in the face of their father or mother and beat them with all their strength. Monks were hustled through the streets handcuffed, with large paper dunces' hats on their heads, and insulted. If you didn't perform convincingly at thamzing, you were beaten by the guards. Many Tibetans lost their hearing as a result of the

During the Cultural Revolution monks and nuns were dragged through the streets of Lhasa with large paper dunces' hats on their heads, insulted and humiliated. © Woeser

numerous blows to their ears, some lost their sight because they were punched in the eyes, and all of them suffered emotional harm during the struggle sessions.

Tendöl was still small when she and her *amala* (mother) were sent for a few months to a road construction camp in Kongpo, near the Indian border. As a member of the upper class, and wife of a former secretary of state, Choekyi was severely punished during the 're-education of the class enemies'. In Kongpo, Choekyi met a woman from Kham who was selling tea near the camp and had a little daughter of her own. She was willing to look after Tendöl. Not far from the camp there was a river and Choekyi was scared that little Tendöl might fall into the torrential stream and drown.

In the camp thamzing took place every evening. The five-year-old girl also attended the struggle sessions. At that age Tendöl did not understand what was going on at all. The cook in the labour camp told her mother that Tendöl sometimes played thamzing all by herself, screaming and hammering on objects with a stick. Choekyi was horrified. 'Even many years later she was unable to talk about it,' recalls Tendöl.

Pema (left): 'If ever something was perfectly conceived to break the soul of a people, it must be these struggle sessions. Only faith in the Dalai Lama and religion saved people from dying. From 1979, under Deng Xiaoping, the strict rules were relaxed a little, the daily thamzing lifted, and families reunited after they had heard nothing from each other for ten or twenty years.'

Mother is Arrested

Tendöl takes her mother's arrest warrant out of an envelope and bursts into tears. Fifty years later, the traumatic event stirs her up as if it had happened the previous day. 'My brother Tenor was already in prison then. My mother and I were back from the camp in the east, and the road was finished. We lived in my aunt's house in Lhasa. It was already dark that December evening when my amala came home. There was a red note on the door. She had no idea why. A little later she looked out of the window and saw a car turning into our narrow alley. She wondered what that might mean. I was sitting on the balcony listening to a Tibetan propaganda broadcast on Chinese radio. We had to listen to such broadcasts every day. Older people often

Choekyi with her three youngest children (around 1962). The 're-education of class enemies' is at its peak.

Tendöl (left) and her friend Doyang, later to be
queen of Mustang.

found this so unbearable that they usually put blankets over
the radios.

'Suddenly I saw many flashlights illuminating our front
door. Chinese military police had come to pick up my
mother. One of them read the warrant in a loud voice. It
said that my mother was an "active counter-revolutionary"
guilty of sabotage. They handcuffed her and searched the
entire apartment. But the Chinese had already looted it
before. All objects of any value had long since disappeared.
My aunt and her daughter, Lochoe, who lived in the

lower apartment, were locked up in the kitchen. I begged my amala: "Take me with you! Don't leave me behind!" Children are not allowed to accompany their arrested parents, shouted a Chinese. I cried, squeezed my way under the barrier to my mother and pulled the chain she was tethered to. My mother called out to me: "Please stop. The prongs are cutting into my skin." The Chinese policemen, accompanied by a Tibetan collaborator, pushed me aside. They locked the apartment, took my amala with them and drove away.'

The next day, Tendöl and her cousin Lochoe went in search of her mother. They took some tea, boiled vegetables and a blanket with them. The girls knew more or less where the prisons were, even if they weren't marked. First, they went to Drapchi prison and asked the guards at the entrance if new prisoners had been admitted but there was no trace of Tendöl's mother. The girls continued their search but could not find her. On their way home, they passed Gutsa prison. There the guards confirmed that Choekyi had indeed been admitted the day before. They asked the guards to at least give the prisoner the food and blanket they had brought with them.

A few days later, Tendöl happened to see her mother being dragged into an office in Lhasa by uniformed officials. She had no way of following her or finding out what had happened to her. It took her several months to be

Tendöl (left) with two friends in Lhasa. The girls have rented traditional chupas to pose in a photographer's studio.

able to visit her amala in prison for the first time. But she was not allowed to talk to her because her mother had not yet been convicted. Once a month, relatives were allowed to take food to the prisoners. Her aunt gave Tendöl a bowl of barley soup for her mother. The little girl was so hungry that she drank some soup on her way to the prison. But on

A. and Tendöl (right). Tendöl: 'A. was my best friend. Her parents were section leaders and therefore our superiors in Lhasa. They were not allowed to talk to us or show that they appreciated us. A. furtively gave me bread when I told her a secret, for example that my mother was in prison or that we had relatives abroad. She often accompanied me when I tried to see my mother in prison.' Tendöl is wearing the striped sweater knitted by her cousin Lochoe.

that day she was refused entry. She should come back in a month, they told her. Disappointed and sad, Tendöl made her way home and was afraid that her aunt would notice that she had furtively eaten a few spoons of soup because she was so hungry.

三组

西藏自治区拉萨市革命委员会人民保卫组

刑 事 判 决 书

（1972）刑 字第17号

现行反革命分子曲吉，女，藏族，现年44岁，家庭领主成份，本人领主分子，城关区东风居委会人，因现行反革命破坏一案，一九七〇年十二月九日依法拘留。

此案业经本组审理终结，现查明：

罪犯曲吉，一九六九年亲自和强迫儿子卡多给叛乱分子扎多等人多次头发、小便、护身符内的东西，卡多穿过的旧衣物一件，母亲穿班禅的红岸心一件，叛乱分子出去后当作叛乱时的护身符，支持了叛乱。同时利用儿子卡多给安尼念经学手段，大肆骗取劳动群众的酥油、羊毛、奶渣和干肉等，一九六九年期间还进行造谣破坏，攻击我党和社会主义制度，妄想复辟万恶的放奴制度。罪犯曲吉经常对其儿子卡多讲印度、不丹和旧社会生活如何好，给儿子卡多灌输资产阶级反动思想。

上述犯罪事实清楚，证据确凿，本人亦供认不讳。

罪犯曲吉，由于长期不接受思想改造，对我党和社会主义制度抱有阶级仇恨，思想反动，但关押后尚能认罪，根据党的"坦白从宽，抗拒从严"的政策精神，经拉萨市革命委员会批准：依法逮捕，判处有期徒刑拾年（刑期从一九七〇年十二月九日起至一九八〇年十二月八日止）。

西藏自治区拉萨市革命委员

人 高 保卫组

一九七二年九月十四日

Translation of Choekyi's sentence (abbreviated)

The active counter-revolutionary Choekyi is Tibetan and currently 44. Her family belongs to the class of feudal lords and she herself is a member of the feudal lords. She was lawfully imprisoned on December 9th, 1970 for active counter-revolution and sabotage.

(. . .) In 1969, the perpetrator Choekyi supported the uprising by repeatedly giving Khado's hair, urine, protective substances and old clothes worn by him as well as a red vest of her mother, worn by Panchen, to the insurgent Tado and others. She also forced her son Khado to do so. The insurgents took these objects and used them as protection amulets during the uprising. Furthermore, with tricks like prayer-recitation for the nomads by her son Khado, she illegally obtained large amounts of butter, wool, cheese and dried meat from the working masses. During 1969, she circulated rumours, sabotaged and attacked our party and our socialist system. She has deluded herself into restoring the satanic system of serfdom. The perpetrator, Choekyi, has repeatedly told her son how beautiful life was in India, Bhutan and in former society and taught her son the reactionary ideology of capitalism.

(. . .) Since the perpetrator Choekyi has not accepted ideological re-education for a long time, opposes our party and our socialist system by class enmity, has reactionary thoughts but has pleaded guilty after her imprisonment, she is, in accordance with the policy of our party which is 'milder treatment to the confessor, severe punishment to the one who denies' (. . .) lawfully arrested and sentenced to ten years imprisonment (the imprisonment period begins on December 9th 1970 and ends on December 8th 1980).

The Revolutionary Committee of Lhasa City of Tibet Autonomous Region. The People's Defense Group September 14th, 1972.

Ten Years in Prison

Tendöl remembers: 'Before the conviction I saw my amala only two or three times. She seemed so fragile in her battered *chupa*, her body trembled all over and she couldn't get a word out. She was utterly scared. Chinese soldiers guarded us armed with pistols and listened to our conversation. After one year, the verdict came: Ten years of hard labour. My mother was transferred to Drapchi prison. We were allowed to visit her depending upon the whims and mood of the Chinese authorities. Usually only once a year. All prisoners were dressed in black. The conversations were prescribed, and at the beginning of each visit we had to recite the same saying: 'We are grateful to China for making a good person out of a bad one.'

Before a prison visit, the Tibetans never knew if their relatives were still alive. If not, they were given a bundle of the deceased's clothes without explanation. When Tendöl went to Drapchi one day, her aunt said: 'If you see your mother, tell her that Tenor has been released.' (Tendöl's brother, Tenor, spent three years in solitary confinement and was released in 1973.) The thirteen-year-old walked as calmly as possible along the prison fence to avoid arousing suspicion. She hoped for some sign from her mother knowing that she was not allowed to talk to her under any circumstances. She saw female prisoners fetching water from the prison yard and immediately recognized her amala, a small, delicate woman whose headscarf was always carefully knotted. She threw a stone to draw her attention and shouted in a loud voice: 'Tenor is home again!' Many years later, her mother told her how happy she had been about this news.

Aunt Yangchen Dolkar heard rumours that Choekyi had been taken to Sera Monastery. Thousands of lamas used to live there but now the monastery served as a prison. Tendöl walked to Sera, an almost two-hour march, and saw a lot of prisoners holding Mao's 'Little Red Book'. She discovered her mother in the crowd but could not approach her. Devastated, she went home again. Almost fifty years later, this story still brings tears to Tendöl's eyes. A few

The Cultural Revolution has devastating consequences for Tibet. A propaganda march in front of Lhasa's Sports Centre. ©Woeser

times, Tendöl saw her amala from afar working outside the prison, for example below Sera Monastery, where the prisoners had to build walls. But not even once could she talk to her, because Tibetans weren't allowed to talk to each other in public.

Tendöl had heard that a Tibetan woman who had been arrested had been shot because she had thrown a spoonful of food over her shoulder to the left and right before each meal—for Buddha and the Dalai Lama. 'I have seen so many dead people buried secretly. Behind Drapchi prison, countless bodies were dumped in mass graves or thrown on a pile', Tendöl says. 'When I tried to visit my mother, I saw men with shovels burying bodies. They were Tibetans guarded by Chinese soldiers. I thought at that time; when Tibet is free again, the world must know this. Over a million Tibetans were killed. Thus, the soul of a people is annihilated.'

Changbi

'When I think of my youth, the images of public executions always come to my mind. They took place three to four times a year, mostly before the Chinese holidays. *Changbi*–execution–was the first Chinese word I learned. I can't erase these images of violence from my memory,' says Tendöl.

She was about eleven. She had to attend the executions because her mother and brother were in prison. She did not want to cause any additional difficulties by not following the rules set by the Chinese. An execution took place one day in the Bo-Lingkha district of Lhasa. The prisoners–exclusively Tibetans–were slowly driven through the streets on trucks. Suddenly, Tendöl saw a woman with long hair and feared at first that it was her mother. The prisoners stood bent forward, their hands tied on their backs and a

Before their execution, prisoners are slowly driven on trucks through Lhasa. Tendöl was forced to attend such executions as a child. ©Woeser

blackboard hung around their necks. If the blackboard was crossed with lines, this meant death by execution. The prisoners wore grey work clothes and all of them looked the same. Tendöl's older sister, Ngodup, who could already read, tried to decipher the names of the prisoners written on the blackboards. When she saw neither her brother nor her mother on the truck, Tendöl ran home and announced the good news. The prisoners who were not executed were

After having been condemned to death . . .

. . . Tibetans are being shot by Chinese soldiers near Lhasa. © Woeser

sentenced to several years in prison. Tibetans were mostly taken away from their homes at night and arrested or killed under some pretext without having committed any crime.

Karma

Chinese brigades came in front of the houses and banged two sticks together. That was the command: The Tibetans had to gather on the street and listen to daily brainwashing. Tibetan collaborators translated from Chinese. The Chinese gave not only political lessons, but also lessons on health and cleanliness.

As a young girl, Tendöl had to publicly curse her father, the former secretary of state, as a bad person, even though she had never met him. The constant drill, the fear, the coercion took their toll on her. Also the fact that she was growing up without her parents, without love and tender care left a deep impact on her. 'I don't know how much a person can endure, but I tried to accept my fate and always believed that the good you do will be given back some day,'

Tendöl (left) around eighteen, with a friend in a photo
studio in Lhasa.

says Tendöl. Although as a butruk she belonged to the
'bad' set of people, she was convinced that she had to make
something good out of her life. According to the Buddhist
teachings on karma, a good deed entails good things, bad

actions bring suffering. 'When you die, the question arises: what have you done with your life? I didn't want to live with that fear.'

Later, in Switzerland, Tendöl read with amazement the letters Dolkar had received from her father. It seemed as if her unknown father had mysteriously transmitted the Buddhist principles to her during the years of suffering. Paljor Jigme Namseling wrote that compassion, kindness and equanimity were the most important commandments in life. One should pray daily for the evil people and for one's enemies. A war could be won quickly, but victory would not last, the father warned. Evil comes back again.

Hunger

After the arrest of her mother Choekyi, Tendöl and her sister, Ngodup, were taken in by their aunt, Yangchen Dolkar. Life became even more precarious for all of them. The aunt had two children left in Tibet, Lochoe and Rigzen. Her husband had been arrested. She could continue to live in her house but she also had to work on the road construction site to survive. She did not earn enough to feed the four children. They all suffered from hunger and were often ill. Food and fuel were almost unavailable in Lhasa. There was hardly any barley, there was no butter, no sugar, no meat—all the traditional main ingredients of Tibetan food. 'If you somehow managed to get a small scrap of butter and you wanted to prepare Tibetan tea, you had to lock your room and pull all your quilts over you so that no one could hear you and denounce you at the next thamzing,'[5] says Tendöl.

Tendöl and her sister were even more isolated than before and lived in constant anguish for their imprisoned mother. Prisoners were regularly dying from exhaustion, disease or execution. Like all Tibetan children, Tendöl and Ngodup were always on a look out for food. They knew that pigs were bred in the Chinese garrisons. The two girls sneaked into the Chinese bases in the evening or during the guards' midday sleep, hid in the pigsty and scooped the food from the troughs into their mouths with their bare hands. Many tried their luck in the garrison of Lhasa; others, such as Tendöl and Ngodup, ran several kilometres to an army camp. The children also looked for a certain plant whose root could be chewed like chewing gum. Tendöl explains, 'We called it *pora yungma,* all the children loved it. The only bad thing was that we often found human remains in the ground when we dug for these roots.'

All Tibetan children also had to kill flies and mosquitoes and deliver a glass of dead insects to the authorities every day. This was a particularly painful task. As a Buddhist, Tendöl had learned to respect all living beings and not to harm them. Now one was forced to kill dogs as well, that too with sticks. Many Tibetans hid their four-legged friends.

---

[5] From cousin Pema's notes after her trip to Lhasa in 1979.

If they were caught, the owners had to kill their dogs with their own hands.

Like many other Tibetan children, Tendöl and her sister Ngodup searched the city for firewood and cow dung from the early days of their childhood. In autumn and winter, many nomads came to Lhasa with their yaks to do business, and the children ran after the animals to collect the flat cakes. When a yak raised its tail in the air, the children shouted as if to announce ownership: 'The excrement of the yak with the white tail is for me.' But not always lucky, sometimes they got showered with urine instead of dung.

This one time they noticed an older man in the neighbourhood who brought his cows, every day, to Ja-Gong-Tang just outside of Lhasa. Their grandmother asked him whether Tendöl and Ngodup could accompany him to collect cow dung on the way. Using a battered bucket and strings grandmother made a rucksack for Tendöl. She found a basket for Ngodup, and from then on, the two girls followed their neighbour and his cattle every day. Ngodup recalls, 'Towards the evening our bags were filled with cow dung, and we headed home. Tendöl was not older than five at that time. She often cried and didn't want to take another step because her backpack was too heavy. I then marched a little ahead, put my basket down and went back to carry Tendöl's pack. It was arduous and we argued until we arrived home. Our grandmother was overjoyed, she gave

Tendöl (left) with a friend in front of the summer palace, the Norbulingka in Lhasa.

us something to eat as a reward and immediately spread the cow dung on the roof of our house to dry.' Ngodup's back and thighs would often swell up from carrying the heavy, damp load. Her grandmother then sewed a small pillow of shredded rags and attached it to the bottom of her basket to protect her back.

At the age of twelve Tendöl was unexpectedly allowed to attend a school in Lhasa. She was taught some writing and arithmetic, but she remembers, above all, the communist propaganda songs they were made to sing every day. She still knows some of them by heart but no longer understands all the words. The slogans were always the same: 'The sun is shining, we are getting up and thanking Mao Zedong . . .' The students were also obliged to go from house to house to collect the cow dung burnt in the ovens, which was used as fertilizer. Before and after school, Tendöl, her cousin Lochoe and her aunt sewed and knit sweaters out of leftover fabric and bits of fur which they collected at a Chinese plant producing uniforms. 'A Muslim Tibetan woman sold the goods for us at the market. We delivered the money to our aunt who used it to buy food,' says Tendöl. Her aunt also secretly taught her the Tibetan script at home and made prostrations with the children in the evening. Tendöl had learnt a few Tibetan prayers from her grandmother. Of course, all this was strictly forbidden.

Tendöl: 'In Tibet the deceased are laid out at home for three days. When our beloved grandmother died, I had to sleep in her bed so that nobody would know that she had died. We were not allowed to cry so that her body could stay in the house.' Ngodup: 'When our grandmother died, my mother feared she would soon be arrested. She told me to sell her sheeps-wool chupa to buy some food.'

'Children are Allowed to Work'

One day the Chinese occupying forces announced: 'Children are allowed to work!' It was no longer a matter of collecting firewood or cow dung, but of proper work organized by the Chinese authorities. Tendöl was assigned to the Jokhang, the most sacred temple in the centre of Lhasa, which was partially destroyed. All Buddha statues had already disappeared. It was said that the Chinese transported the copper the statues contained all the way to China to manufacture cartridges. The Tibetan children had to clean and tidy up. Everywhere they noticed traces of blood. Tendöl heard that Tibetans had been murdered in the Jokhang by nails being pierced into their heads . . .

Tendöl smiling, surrounded by rhododendron bushes. This picturesque image was taken during the hard years of road building in Kongpo.

the brutality was boundless. This was the time after Mao's death when the Gang of Four tried to seize power in China.

After almost two years Tendöl was thrown out of school and assigned to a road construction group. As a butruk she was promised that she could complete an apprenticeship two years later. As expected, the promise was not kept, she spent almost five years at the road construction camp of Po-Tramo. Together with many, mostly Chinese youths,

Tendöl (front row far right) with her colleagues in Kongpo. In bad weather, the road-builders had a day off from time to time.

she was taken on a three-day bus trip to Kongpo near the border with India. Chinese youths also had to work on road construction in order to obtain the right to attend school or to receive vocational training. They were divided into groups of 400; there were not more than two or three Tibetans per group. Tendöl had friendly relations with her Chinese companions and, thanks to them, was better fed in

Po-Tramo than in the usual all-Tibetan labour camps. They received work attire and were able to wash in the evening. They lived in large tents, had to build their own wooden bedsteads and were guarded day and night by soldiers. In the yellowing photos, amidst rhododendron bushes, Tendöl seemed to be in pretty good shape and looks surprisingly robust. 'We spent a lot of time outdoors and had enough exercise,' she remarks, ironically.

But the work was hard. Girls and boys had to chisel, blast, carry or smash stones day in, day out. The only free time they got was when the weather was so bad they couldn't work. Hundreds of young people died of exhaustion or injuries and were buried on the spot. Tendöl's hands were always sore. Once a nail had penetrated her foot; hardly able to walk, she still had to work.

The road blasted through the steep mountain gorges of Po-Tramo was a secret government project involving five brigades of soldiers and workers, each with over 5,000 people. The Chinese not only built roads, they cut whole forested mountains bare and transported the timber to China. After a few years the huge area became completely barren, Tendöl recalls. In contrast to Lhasa, this area in Kongpo bore dense forests. In the past, it was said, you could ride here for days without seeing the sky. The region was rich in apricots, and the meat of the wild boars supposedly tasted like apricots. The Chinese had created an environmental destruction of mammoth dimensions. Kongpo was practically deforested then. The rich vegetation of this southern Tibetan landscape disappeared forever.

During all those years Tendöl could not confide in anyone. She told no one that her mother was in prison and pretended that her aunt was her mother. In the tent, she slept like a foetus with her legs and arms gripped tight to protect herself. She overcame this habit but many years later. She still hasn't forgotten how she cried herself to sleep every night until the pillow was completely soaked.

Ngodup (right): 'I had many sad experiences, the hard work as a child, the death of my beloved grandmother, the arrest of my brother and mother. But the saddest memory, which I still feel like a stab in my heart, was when Tendöl was sent to Kongpo to work on road construction. Even today I cry when I think about it.'

She longed for her beloved amala, of whom she had heard nothing for ages. She hid the photos of her family in her belongings. But she never gave up. She fought and tried to do good deeds so that her mother would survive in prison. She got up earlier than the other inmates and lit the fire. In the evening, she boiled water and prepared the footbath of the Chinese guards. Together with a Chinese girl she distributed the food. Like all the other camp inmates, she had a card with her achievements on it. Tendöl is the most industrious, it said. But it did her no good, because she was a Tibetan and a butruk on top of that.

Mao Zedong died on 9 September 1976. Tendöl had heard days before from her Chinese colleagues in the camp that the 'Great Helmsman' was seriously ill. Among the Tibetans, someone owned a small transistor radio, and they all searched for information in Chinese broadcasts. They heard funeral music everywhere and saw the Chinese in tears. 'We understood that we Tibetans also had to cry to avoid problems, even though the news of Mao's death actually brought joy to our hearts,' Tendöl recalls. They rubbed sand and dust in their eyes and the trick worked. The Tibetan youths who were supposed to build roads cried as bitterly as the Chinese and in Mao's honour they also attached a white wool rose to their work clothes, and wore a black ribbon around their left upper arm.

After his escape from Tibet, Paljor Jigme Namseling first works in Kalimpong (India) and then in Gangtok (Sikkim) as a representative of the Dalai Lama. After his retirement, he spends his final years with his daughter Soyang in Gangtok. He dies in 1973, heartbroken.

In the fall of 1979, Tendöl and two Tibetan girls from the work brigades in Kongpo spent a Chinese holiday in the nearby town of Po-Tramo. There they met a group of men wearing traditional Tibetan chupas. On hearing the girls speak Tibetan, one of them asked, 'Are you from Lhasa?' They replied, 'Yes.' 'What are Lhasa girls doing in such a remote place?' a man wondered. On finding out that Tendöl was Namseling's daughter, they told her that he had passed away. Tendöl was immediately in tears. They gave each of the girls 200 Yuan (approximately three months' wages in road construction).

The girls understood that these Tibetans had come from India and they were overjoyed, recalls Tendöl. But it never occurred to them that they had met the first Tibetan fact-finding delegation to Tibet sent by the Dalai Lama. Amongst the members were the Dalai Lama's brother, Lobsang Samten, and also his brother-in-law. Chinese officials later questioned the girls intensively about what had been said. Tendöl told them that her father had died but never admitted that they had received money which would have entailed a severe punishment.

Choekyi is Free

The year was 1979. Tendöl had just turned twenty and was still working on the road construction site. One day she received a letter from Lhasa: 'Mother has been released from prison.' Choekyi had spent nine years and eleven months behind bars and in labour camps and Tendöl was finally given permission to travel to Lhasa to visit her. Hitchhiking was the only way to get there, but it was not safe for a young girl. With the savings from her meagre wages as a road builder, she bought cigarettes for the Chinese drivers who offered to take her part of the way and spent the nights in small Chinese hotels along the road.

In Lhasa, she could finally embrace her beloved amala. Her happiness knew no bounds, but sadly, mother and daughter met each other almost as strangers. Tendöl had

Choekyi after her release. In 1979 her niece Pema meets her in Lhasa: 'When I arrived at my mother's house, my aunt came towards me with an auspicious bow. My relatives were in a small room. Then the tears really came. The shock of seeing how the years of hunger, fear and hard work had battered my relatives was almost greater than the joy of being reunited with them. Choekyi, my mother's younger sister, had been released from prison a few weeks earlier. She was only 51 but looked like 70. But she still had the same smile and the same mischievous eyes. Everybody had broken teeth, even the young ones. Many had only two or three teeth left and no way to replace the gaps.'

been ten-years-old when her mother was arrested before her eyes. Ten years had passed since then. Both had to find a new intimacy and deal with the pain of separation, and the years of deprivation. Choekyi, the beautiful young woman, had aged prematurely. Her face and her stunted body showed traces of the time she had spent in prison; she was in bad health. But she was alive and had been released on parole a month earlier than scheduled in the sentence.

This unexpected 'leniency' was mainly due to the fact that Choekyi's eldest daughter, Soyang, got married to the youngest son of the ruler of Sikkim[6], the Eleventh Chögyal, and her niece Pema visited Lhasa at that time. Tendöl and her mother hardly had time to tell each other what they had experienced over the past decade. After less than two weeks, the reunion with her amala was already over. Tendöl had to return to the construction site in Kongpo. Choekyi moved back into the apartment in Lhasa where she had lived before her arrest.

Shortly afterwards Tendöl received good news again; she was allowed to start an apprenticeship as a motor mechanic in Lhasa! 'I had been eagerly awaiting this opportunity for years. Finally, I was allowed to learn something. It was my happiest time in Tibet,' she says. She worked in a large

---

[6] The Chögyals (tib. Dharma King) have been monarchs of the former kingdom of Sikkim since 1642. In 1975, the monarchy was abolished following a referendum and Sikkim was incorporated into India.

Choekyi with Tendöl (left), Ngodup and her son. Reunited and happy that their mother had survived prison.

Top: Tendöl (second from left) dancing with a girlfriend in Norbulingka park. Bottom: Tendöl (centre) poses with colleagues and their Chinese instructors during the apprenticeship.

Top: Tendöl (second from right) with her colleagues during her apprenticeship as a car mechanic.

Bottom: Tendöl (front row, third from right) with Tibetan apprentices and drivers in Lhasa.

car repair enterprise with hundreds of employees, most of them Chinese. N., her friend from the road construction, completed the apprenticeship with her. An accident had brought the two girls particularly close together: When N. severely injured her arm in an explosion, Tendöl cared for her as well as she could in the Po-Tramo camp, and ended up forming an unbreakable bond.

Tenor Khado, the Brother

Tenor, whose full name is Tenzin Norbu Namseling, was recognized by His Holiness the Dalai Lama at the age of three as the incarnation of the fifth Khado Rinpoche, a sacred lama of the Tibetan tradition. As he was too young to enter the monastery he was allowed to grow up at home for the time being.

Before being arrested, Choekyi lived with her three youngest children in the house of her sister Yangchen Dolkar in Lhasa. She used to hide the family photos in the roof beams. Through some secret channel, she had received pictures of her husband and her three daughters living in Kalimpong. She asked her son Tenor to hide these pictures

Tendöl's brother Tenor at his enthronement as Sixth Khado Rinpoche aged three (1957).

in his jacket. Shortly afterwards Tenor was arrested. He was sixteen-years-old.

This happened in 1970. The Cultural Revolution had been raging in China for four years. The campaign against 'counter-revolutionary elements' and the reign of terror of the Red Guards, also spread in Tibet. Tendöl heard someone scream: 'Bring tea and *tsampa* to the authorities. Tenor has been arrested . . . ' But Tenor had already been taken away. The whole family was worried sick and hoped that he had swallowed the family photos sent from India. Suddenly Choekyi noticed that Tenor had forgotten his jacket at home. The authorities ordered her to bring his clothes to prison. Everyone was so excited and frightened that they forgot to remove the photos from the jacket. In prison, it wasn't long before the guards discovered them. Tenor was already in chains and the first of many endless interrogations revolved around the origin of these photos.

Tenor spent three years in prison[7]–in solitary confinement. His punishment was particularly severe because he not only came from a noble family but also was a Buddhist monk. During the first two weeks, his hands were tied day and night on his back. Large steel locks on his back and his chest prevented him from lying down. When the handcuffs were removed, his arms were in such pain that he could no longer move them. For the eight months his feet were tied together with heavy iron chains he could neither wash nor change clothes. The food was pushed into his cell through a small gap under the door. He approached the bowl on all fours, pushed it onto the mattress with his bound feet, bent as low as he could and slurped the food down. 'This achievement made me really proud and regularly gave me some exercise,' he said years later.

Tenor was interrogated every day. He was accused of having planned an uprising, supposedly incited by his mother. They threatened to kill his mother, who had

---

[7] *Lost Legacy*, Elizabeth Bayard Winter, Tricycle Magazine, New York, 1991.

been arrested in the meantime. From then on his mother appeared to him every night in a dream. He heard her voice and feared that she would be killed. Soon he heard voices all the time; he thought that he was losing his mind and wanted to kill himself. From the small box that served as a latrine, he dropped to the floor. But he was not dead. He unscrewed the light bulb in his cell and put a finger in it. Nothing happened because he was standing on the wooden box.

Tenor Khado in front of the Potala, a few months before leaving Tibet for India (approx. 1983/84).

He broke a window pane and shouted: 'Please kill me'. His tormentors came to the cell the night after this breakdown. He was brutally beaten until he fainted. Cold water was poured over him. When he regained consciousness, he was dripping wet and frozen. He was desperate. Why did he have to suffer so much? He was only sixteen and had never harmed anyone. He pleaded to heaven but got no answer.

Slowly he plucked up courage again. He imagined that the Chinese would change over time and not oppress his country anymore. He had seen many executions and heard of many Tibetans committing suicide by shooting themselves or jumping into the river flowing through Lhasa. He prayed that no other country would suffer such a reign of terror.

During the three years of solitary confinement he could not speak to any other prisoner. So, he began to communicate with the birds circling above the prison, often in a small weed-covered corner between a wall and his window. 'I soon understood their language, for example when they told the other birds that they had found a worm. I understood when they were content or arguing with each other. Every bird had a friend, and I knew who belonged to whom, except for a one-legged bird that was always alone', Tenor said many years later in the USA.

He also prayed that his mother would not be executed and that his two younger sisters would survive. As a political

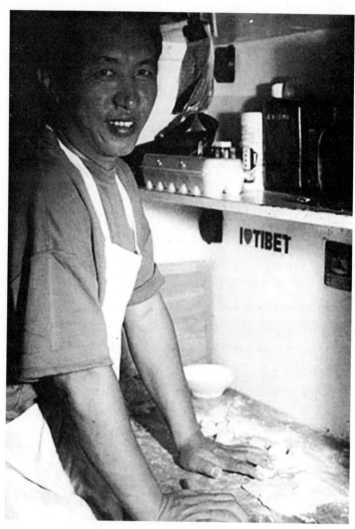

In 1984 Tenor is also allowed to leave Tibet. He first works in 'Tibet Kitchen' in Manhattan, New York. Today he lives with his family near Washington, D.C.

prisoner, he had to study newspapers and books written by Mao, Marx, Engels and Lenin translated into Tibetan and he had to write down his 'progress' every week. He was given a crossed-out blackboard which meant that his execution was already planned. But Tenor survived and, to this day, believes that Sungma, his protective goddess[8] who appeared to him every night in a dream, saved him then.

One day he was called to the prison warden's office and was told–without any explanation–that he would be released on the spot and that his mother was still alive but had been sentenced to ten years in prison. He received a ration card and was not allowed to leave Lhasa. The sixth Khado, destined for a holy life in a monastery, now worked in a quarry but at least he was no longer tortured in prison.

Almost ten years later, in 1982, the protracted efforts of Tenor's sisters Soyang, Dolkar, Tenzing and his cousin Pema were rewarded with success. Choekyi and her youngest daughters Ngodup and Tendöl received permission to leave the country. Only Tenor had to stay in Tibet. He served as a hostage that could be used, depending on the behaviour of his relatives in exile. Tenor was not allowed to leave the country until 1984. He emigrated to the USA and started to work in a Tibetan restaurant in New York. Today he lives

---

[8] When he travelled, many years later, from his American exile to Tibet, he saw for the first time an image of Sungma in the Kardo nunnery near Lhasa.

Left: Tendöl and Dolkar, the wife of her uncle in Kathmandu. Right: Ngodup and Tendöl (right) after leaving Tibet in 1981. They travel with their mother to Dharamsala via Nepal and later fly to Switzerland.

with his wife, Niyma Youdon, who practises traditional Tibetan medicine, and their two children in Washington, where he works as a driver. Tenor never spoke about the time spent in prison again, not even with his sisters or his mother.

In 2016 Tenor travelled back to Tibet. Nomads came in droves to visit him. The rumour 'Khado is back' spread like wildfire. Thirty years of Chinese rule had not eradicated the Buddhist faith. But Tenor reassured his fellow Tibetans:

'I'm just a layman; in the quarry I had a hammer in my hands instead of a notebook and a pen.' In America he was asked if he felt like an incarnation. He said, 'I don't know. Yes and no. The Dalai Lama recognized me as the sixth Khado Rinpoche. He must know. I can't decide about that. I don't remember anything.' He added that 'criticism is also part of Buddhism' and that he 'believes in Buddha, but by interpreting religion in a dogmatic way, people have caused many misunderstandings'.

Namseling Manor

Namseling Manor is a seven-storey seventeeth century building, the ancestral family estate on the southern bank of the Brahmaputra River. Tendöl's older sister, Dolkar, recalls: 'We went on holiday to Namseling Manor once or twice a year, often playing outdoors and stealing food from the fields. We travelled on the Brahmaputra in a boat made of yak leather. If we had to stop at night, we secured the boat to the shore with a rope. Our escort stayed ashore and we slept in the boat with our mother. It was quite adventurous.'

Namseling Manor is listed by the 'World Monuments Watch'. A watchtower, Buddhist murals, a prayer room, a Tibetan Lingka garden with flowers, poplars, apple and nut trees make Namseling Manor a rare example of Tibetan

Namseling Manor; in 2006 Choekyi travels to Tibet and visits her family's former estate on the banks of the Kyi Chu (Brahmaputra).

Choekyi and her niece Pema perform a farewell 'village dance' with Bhuti (centre), the family's former nanny.

architecture in the traditional style of a 'residence for the god of wealth'. The building has so far been spared decay; the structure has been stabilized and an entrance gate has been added. But the plan to establish a cultural centre at Namseling Manor will probably never materialize.

In 2006 Choekyi travelled to Tibet with her niece, Pema. They visited the former family estate, Namseling Manor and met some former employees, including Bhuti, who had worked as a nanny in the Namseling household for many years. They drank butter tea and *chang* (Tibetan barley beer) in Bhuti's house. Before saying goodbye, Bhuti wanted to sing and dance like in olden times. With tears in her eyes, Choekyi took part in the so-called 'village dance'. She had brought gifts and medicine for the people living around Namseling Manor.

In Lhasa, Choekyi also met former acquaintances from prison. They were no longer prisoners, but as Tibetans they were not free in their own country. After six weeks in Tibet, Choekyi and her niece could no longer stand the oppressive atmosphere and flew back to Nepal.

Choekyi is Reunited With her Children

'My amala had become a completely different person. She still had the same voice and the same kind eyes, but she looked like my grandmother', Dolkar describes the reunion in 1982 with her mother at Pestalozzidorf, Trogen, after a separation of almost twenty-five years. The poverty, the hard work, the imprisonment and the constant fear for her three children who remained with her in Tibet had prematurely turned the blooming Choekyi into an old, stooped woman. Dolkar and Tenzing also met their youngest sister, Tendöl, for the first time. She was like a stranger from Tibet but

The whole Namseling family, including Tenor, is reunited in Switzerland in 1994. Only missing is their father who died twenty-one years earlier. Above: Tendöl front right. Below: Visiting Dolkar and Tenzing at the Pestalozzi Village.

looked so similar to them, with the typical features of the Namseling family. Her hair was braided into a thick plait, and she was still wearing her cheap Chinese clothes from Lhasa. Ngodup accompanied her, the second youngest sister who had seen Dolkar and Tenzing for the last time back in 1958, when they had travelled to Kalimpong together with their mother.

Choekyi didn't talk much about the past two and a half decades; sometimes she almost casually made a small remark, 'Oh yes, in those days . . .'. And when she did talk, she only mentioned fragments from the past. As if the terrible events could not be conjured up at all in the peaceful world of Switzerland. Everything seemed almost unreal, incomprehensible in this perfect environment. How could she find words to describe the suffering and cruelty she had experienced and seen in Tibet? Choekyi never revealed her deepest spiritual and physical pain. 'We did not question her, it was too painful,' Dolkar explains. 'They first lived with us in the Pestalozzi Village. Our two children were still small at that time. Like almost all newly-emigrated Tibetans, my mother and sisters wanted to return to Tibet. "The Chinese occupation would last a few years at most," they thought–just like all of us. Over time we found a way to cope with everyday life, but it wasn't easy.'

In Switzerland, Choekyi prayed and meditated several hours a day. She made it her daily practise to recite the entire

Above: Choekyi in her youth, and below, in later years, smiling and with mischievous eyes despite her hard life.

Tibetan prayer book. Faith had kept her alive all these years and she had no feelings of anger or bitterness. Everyone loved her dearly, her hearty laughter, her gentleness and her sense of humour. She was quick-witted in reminding her grandchildren, 'You think that you know everything better than us old people. Do not forget that we have experienced a lot more.' Once she played a Tibetan song on her old-fashioned mobile phone. It was about the fate of their lost country. Tendöl's daughter, Tenzin Kelden, saw her grandmother wiping away tears as a profound sadness came over her. 'When I asked her about my mother's childhood, I always felt how deep her grief was,' says the granddaughter. 'Her husband had to flee Tibet, she never saw him again; three of her daughters went to school in India, and she had to abandon her three youngest children in Lhasa when she was arrested. So much pain is almost unbearable for a mother.' Tendöl's son, Jigmi, remembers falling asleep on his grandmother's lap. 'We didn't have long conversations. My Tibetan was anything but perfect, but grandmother was an incredible person. She was always cheerful and had a lightness of spirit that allowed her to distance herself from the past. Thus, she protected herself and made things much easier for us too.'

There are also cheerful anecdotes from this period. Tendöl and Choekyi once again visited Dolkar and Tenzing in the Pestalozzi Village. In her 'other life', when she and her children suffered from hunger in Tibet, Choekyi had exchanged a jade ring for *tsampa* (barley flour). When the trader, half Nepalese, half Tibetan, had permission to travel abroad, he went to Sikkim to see Choekyi's eldest daughter, Soyang. He told her: 'This ring belonged to your mother, she exchanged it for barley.' Dolkar saw the ring when she visited Soyang many years later and took it with her to Switzerland. Suddenly, during a meal at Pestalozzidorf, Choekyi asked: 'Dolkar, where did you get that ring from?' 'A merchant brought it to Soyang in Sikkim and told her that it belonged to you. Soyang bought it back from him and gave it to me.' Dolkar still wears this ring every day. Despite the closed borders, and the impossibility of communication, this jade ring had reached Choekyi's daughters abroad like a miraculous sign of life from their mother who had 'disappeared' in Tibet.

In spite of the happy reunion with her children and grandchildren in Switzerland and the USA, Choekyi felt most comfortable in Dharamsala, surrounded by Tibetan culture, in the company of exiled older Tibetans and close to His Holiness the Dalai Lama. She lived there for a few years in simple circumstances, had no material needs and did not wish to own anything anymore. Her mind was at peace but her health was deteriorating. So her family took her to a hospital in Mumbai (where Soyang's daughter, Gawa, lives). Three Tibetan lamas were invited too, and Choekyi's children and grandchildren all travelled to Mumbai to accompany her on her last journey. She died in 2013 at the age of eighty-three. As her mother had wished, Soyang, the eldest daughter, organized a dignified Tibetan funeral in Sikkim, just as she had done forty years earlier for her father, Paljor Jigme. Choekyi's body was cremated in the midst of the beautiful mountain landscape. Tenor, her only son, set the pyre alight. Dozens of white prayer-flags fluttered in the wind. Choekyi's ashes were scattered in the river.

Tendöl praying in front of her mother's ashes in Sikkim.

Switzerland, Another Planet

Tendöl travelled to Switzerland in 1982 carrying a cheap brown Chinese travel bag and a few belongings. She wore a green padded anorak. She has kept both objects carefully at home until today, as if she sometimes had to prove to herself that a long time ago she arrived here from a 'different world', almost miraculously. She applied for asylum in Switzerland. Her name was spelt as 'Zhuoma Danzen' in her passport, a Chinese citizen. On one hand, the Chinese could not pronounce her Tibetan name, and on the other hand, Tendöl was reluctant to divulge the Namseling family name, so scorned by the Chinese.

Tendöl was most unhappy in Switzerland. She experienced an overwhelming conflict between the two cultures. With her best friends far away, she felt lost in this foreign land. Her two sisters, Dolkar and Tenzing, had lovingly welcomed and sheltered her, but they met each other for the first time and up until then their lives had been completely different.

Tendöl was torn. She wanted to go back to Tibet, back to her friend from the days of road construction. She loved him and wanted to marry him but could not confide her secret to anyone, because intimate relationships were not allowed in Tibet before marriage. She still keeps the Chinese ballpoint pen, her friend's farewell gift. Tendöl had suddenly landed in a paradise of material prosperity and could not cope with the Swiss lifestyle. She wanted to leave. But going back to Tibet was not possible, and wouldn't be as long as the country was not free. She dreamed of the USA and even received a visa. Before her departure she was asked at the Zurich airport if she wanted to stay in the USA forever. Naively, she answered 'Yes' and promptly her entry was withdrawn.

So, she had to stay in Switzerland. Dolkar found her a job as a cleaning lady in the district hospital in Baden, near Zurich. 'In Tibet I had finally received vocational training and I loved my job as a motor mechanic. In Switzerland I had to clean toilets. It was awful,' recalls Tendöl. She also cleaned the apartment of two male medical doctors and one day saw the two kissing. The shock was profound. What kind of world was that? She didn't know what to do. She recalls standing on a bridge over the River Limmat, dithering. Should she jump into the water or not? Only the embarrassing thought of someone pulling out her drowned body stopped her from taking the extreme step.

But she wanted to be independent. Tendöl found a job in the household of a well-to-do family in Bern and also attended a housekeepers' school and spent the weekends with another family in Bern itself. There she met Chungtag, an adopted Tibetan who was to become her husband.

Marriage and Children

She married Chungtag in 1986. Both were Tibetans, but had grown up in two different worlds and had to build their lives between two different cultures. Chungtag had been brought to Switzerland as a small boy in the early sixties under the 'Aeschimann children' initiative, and was taken in by a Swiss family in Bern. Tendöl spent her childhood in Tibet in fear, loneliness and labour camps. Chungtag clearly remembers the panic attacks which Tendöl sometimes experienced. During a walk in the Bremgarten forest near Bern, she told him in all seriousness that in case of an emergency they would have to run away from the bears in a zigzag pattern. It was in the Po-Tramo camp that she had

Tendöl with Chungtag and their two children in Bern.

witnessed farmers being attacked by bears, and fleeing for their lives.

Tenzin Kelden was born in 1986 and Jigmi three years later. Tendöl and Chungtag were overjoyed, but their marriage did not last. The two separated but have remained good friends to this day. Tendöl fought hard for her family. She wanted her children to receive the best possible education, something she had been denied.

In Erlach, Moosseedorf and various other places near Bern, she set up market stalls, often at Christmas too, selling goods which her cousin Pema and her sister Soyang sent from India and Nepal, or which she purchased from her friends at Tibet House in Basel. Sometimes she also received items from Dharamsala from her mother Choekyi.

In 1996 a big dream came true: along with two other partners, Tendöl founded her own shop, Lhasa Boutique, at Münstergasse in Bern's old town. Over the years the shop has become a meeting place for Tibet friends, a small Tibetan oasis in the city. Since 2016, she has been running the business alone–with the active support of her family: 'For me, the Lhasa Boutique is much more than just a business. It is a place where I can meet my fellow human beings with an open heart and give them a little joy.'

Tendöl with her daughter, Tenzin Kelden, who has become an important partner in the family business since 2016. 'My mother is one of the strongest people I know. We know what she went through and how she had to fight – finally I get the opportunity to give her back something.'

Tendöl with her two children.

Tenzin Kelden works for the Migros-Kulturprozent in Zurich and has a Master's degree in Social Sciences. She would like to be more creative and initiate new projects with her partner, Dhondup. Since 2017, she has been campaigning for Tibetans to develop an independent film language as a member of the organizing committee of the Tibet Film Festival, Zurich. 'We Tibetans have to tell our own stories. It's a form of resistance.'

Jigmi has been working in digital marketing at Swisscom since 2016. He holds a Bachelor of Science degree in Business Administration and Corporate Communications & Marketing. He owes his professional success above all to his parents. 'As a boy, I was full of mischief and sometimes my grades were pretty bad. Our education was extremely important to my mother and she did everything she could to motivate me.' Jigmi is married to Tenphün, a dentist and second-generation Tibetan. They have a little daughter called Tashi Pema.

A Stranger in Her
Own Country

At the turn of the millennium, Tendöl travelled with her former business partner to Kathmandu to buy goods for the shop. Due to unrest, all businesses were closed in Nepal and the two Tibetan women (with Swiss passports) decided to travel onward to Tibet. They managed to get visas and bought presents for Tendöl's aunt, Lungsher. When their plane landed in Lhasa, and Tendöl saw Chinese soldiers on the tarmac, she started to tremble violently and cry because she was so scared.

They spent a week in Lhasa. Most of her old acquaintances[9] had learnt Chinese and some were employed

---

[9] To protect Tendöl's acquaintances in Lhasa, their names are not mentioned.

Tendöl with a former neighbour in Lhasa.

in the Chinese administration. Materially, they were doing relatively well, but they were afraid and hardly talked about their lives under Chinese rule. There were rats in the house. At night, they appeared even in the bedroom. 'We had no rats before, the Chinese brought them to Tibet,' Tendöl notes with disgust.

She also visited a few friends from her years working in the road construction and from her apprenticeship as a motor mechanic. A childhood friend invited her home. Tendöl recalls, 'We drank tea with her parents and everybody started to cry. In her living room, I discovered an old photo of me.'

She hardly recognized Lhasa. Many buildings in the old town had disappeared. The former two-storey house of her aunt now had four floors. An old man she knew from before still lived there. The tax office for Lhasa was now located in her parents' former house. The old vegetable market was full of Chinese products, and many Chinese sat at long tables playing mahjong. 'Everything looked just like China. The Potala had become a museum full of tourists. I felt like a stranger in my own country. I belonged to the oppressed minority. This journey was the end of my longing that had been drawing me back to Tibet all these years,' says Tendöl today, and if she feels a bout of melancholy she doesn't let it show.

Second Marriage

Since 2006, Tendöl has been married to Tseten Samdup Chhoekyapa, one of the secretaries to the fourteenth Dalai Lama. Having spent twenty-five years in Europe, Tseten returned to India in 2016, to work for His Holiness the Dalai Lama in Dharamsala, accompanying him on his trips abroad. Tseten grew up in a refugee camp and attended a school for Tibetan refugees in India. Thanks to a scholarship, he completed his higher education at a Jesuit college in Darjeeling and later studied at Columbia University, New York.

Tseten has never been to Tibet, but he knows the history and political situation of his homeland in depth. 'The political situation in Tibet is irreversible,' he says without hesitation. 'China is a modern colonial regime.

His Holiness the Dalai Lama's Middle Way Approach–*umaylam*–does not seek independence, but genuine autonomy within the framework of the People's Republic of China. Unfortunately, China rejected this proposal. (i.e. Tibet would remain part of the People's Republic of China, but Tibetans would have meaningful autonomy). During the Cultural Revolution in China, from 1966 to 1976, a great deal of Tibetan culture was destroyed. Under these conditions, it was almost impossible to preserve the national identity.' Many young Tibetans are now studying in China, because they can find no jobs in Tibet without being literate in Chinese. 'But even after seventy years of occupation, the Chinese have not succeeded in winning the hearts and minds of the Tibetans or in breaking their spirit of resistance.

'As a child of the frowned-upon elite, Tendöl lost all rights. It was pushed down her throat that her father and mother were bad people. Her mother and her brother were in prison, her father was ostracized as a "bloodsucker", a representative of the Tibetan government and the upper class. She grew up with a deep-seated fear; the psychological consequences of such a childhood never fade away. Tendöl sometimes has flashbacks, she has panic attacks that we can hardly understand. Like her mother, she survived this time by believing in Buddhist principles; things come and go, nothing is permanent. What we have lost is not important if we don't hang on to it. If you are honest, friendly and open, your life will be good. Despite her terrible childhood and youth, Tendöl has remained a kind and generous person. She has found her way in a foreign culture and has succeeded in giving her children an excellent education.'

Tendöl with Tseten, her second husband.

Faith

As a small child in Lhasa, Tendöl had secretly learnt a few Tibetan prayers with her grandmother. Her mother was too scared to commit such an act of disobedience. The practise of her faith was strictly forbidden during her youth and still is today in Tibet under Chinese occupation. And yet she only survived the years of turmoil because she internalized the principles of Buddhism and never lost the belief that the good that one does comes back.

'I never really learnt the Tibetan prayers', Tendöl says regretfully. But she has found a way that allows her to pray daily: YouTube! 'I prefer to listen to the philosophical teachings of the Dalai Lama or the meditations of

On the occasion of an audience in Dharamsala (1981), His Holiness the Dalai Lama gave this picture to Tendöl with the dedication that he would include her in his prayers. He called her father, Paljor Jigme, 'a good man who fully committed himself to Tibet.' Tendöl was overjoyed. She had only heard bad things about her father from the Chinese.

Shantideva[10], especially the chapters on patience and anger. That has always helped me to solve problems in my life,'

---

[10] Shantideva, a monk and son of a king, lived in the eighth century to the north of Bodhgaya and is regarded as the author of the 'Bodhicharyavatara' (a guide to cultivating the mind of enlightenment) and of 'Shikshasamuccaya' (a collection of rules), the great classics of Mahayana Buddhism which explain the ethics of a Bodhisattva. According to Tibetan Buddhism, Shantideva can guide disciples approaching him with unswerving trust.

explains Tendöl. Just like the teachings of the Dalai Lama, which she attended every time he visited Switzerland, as well as during the annual gatherings and solemn religious meetings of Tibetans in Bodhgaya. She draws great strength from her love for her two children and their father, her husband Tseten, her family, her friends and the people she meets.

Epilogue

The story of Tendöl's childhood is only one among countless others that remain unheard. It symbolizes the tragic fate of the Tibetan population after the Chinese seized the country. Tendöl had the opportunity to begin a new life in exile. Around 110,000 Tibetans who managed the dangerous journey on foot across the Himalayas to Dharamsala also had the same 'luck'. But thousands of other Tibetans who tried to escape to India, Nepal or Bhutan died or were arrested while fleeing.

The record of the Chinese occupation is tragic. One fifth of the six million Tibetans were victims of repression or starved to death. Countless children were separated from their families and interned in Chinese orphanages for 're-education'. Two million nomads have been expelled from their original homelands and resettled in desolate barracks in order to give way to Beijing's exploitation of natural resources, with catastrophic consequences for the environment. Tibetan institutions and traditions are systematically annihilated, while Buddhism is described as a 'disease to be eradicated'. Monasteries have been destroyed or closed down and thousands of monks and nuns suffered prison terms. Today Lhasa is overwhelmingly a Chinese city, the Potala a tourist attraction and the Tibetans are a minority in their own homeland.

Tibet, to this day, remains one of the most repressive countries in the world. The Tibetan flag, a picture of the Dalai Lama, a song about freedom or a peaceful demonstration can result in years of imprisonment. Therefore, the resistance that continues to this day is all the more remarkable. Young Tibetans, whose parents or even grandparents know nothing but a life under Chinese rule, take part in protests against oppression. This resistance is mostly non-violent in accordance to the philosophy and guidance of the Dalai Lama. Over the last ten years, at least 150 Tibetan men, women and youths have chosen to die through self-immolation. 10 March, the historic day of the 1959 uprising, has been the trigger for several huge protests. In 2008, a few months before the Olympic Games in Beijing, violent riots broke out throughout the country against the Chinese occupiers. The suppression was brutal, as always. Today, Xi Jinping, the Chinese president-for-life, promises to relentlessly fight 'Tibetan separatism'.

The fate of the Tibetans carries little weight in view of the realpolitik imposed worldwide. This book is an opportunity to recall events that have been taking place on the 'roof of the world' for seven decades and are rarely mentioned in our news, due largely to China's information blockade.

Chronology

1935

Birth of Lhamo Thondup, recognized as the fourteenth
   Dalai Lama, son of a peasant family in the province of
   Amdo. A search party identifies him as the reincarnation
   of the thirteenth Dalai Lama at the age of two.

1940

As a four-year-old, the Dalai Lama is enthroned in Lhasa as
   spiritual leader of six million Tibetans.

1944

Choekyi and Paljor Jigme Namseling, Tendöl's parents, get
   married.

1950

Mao Zedong declares the 'peaceful liberation' of Tibet and announces to solve the political conflict through 'reunification with the Motherland'. In October, 40,000 PLA soldiers invade and occupy the Kham area. Around 8,000 members of the Tibetan resistance force, Chushi Gangdruk, fight against the invaders in the following years. On 17 November, at only fifteen years, the Dalai Lama is asked to assume political leadership. The Tibetan government is made up of around 500 civil servants, half of whom are monks and the rest representatives of the country's 200 aristocratic families. A unified political strategy is lacking.

1951

China forces the Tibetan government, under duress, to sign the '17-Point Agreement for the Peaceful Liberation of Tibet' in Beijing. This surrenders Tibet to China, but religious freedom, monasteries and the role of the Dalai Lama will be retained. At that moment, Mao Zedong is pursuing a 'gradual strategy' of integration into the Chinese state in the hope that the Tibetans will accept China's occupation. Around 8,000 Chinese military and civil servants are stationed in Lhasa, while the Tibetan capital has between 30,000 and 40,000 inhabitants prior to the PLA arrival.

Jigme Paljor Namseling mistrusts the '17-Point Agreement', which in reality provides for the annexation of Tibet to China. Like a majority of Tibetans, he does not regard the PLA as a liberator but as an alien occupier.

1952

The Central Committee of the Chinese Communist Party takes direct control of Tibet; all decisions must first be approved in Beijing.

Paljor Namseling belongs to a secret group of influential men who have set themselves the goal of fighting the Chinese occupation by all means. The Tibetan People's Association, founded in Lhasa, petitions the military occupiers. The document, in which Paljor Jigme presumably played a key role, calls for 'improving relations between the Chinese and Tibetans' in six points. Under these conditions, Tibet would have become a kind of Chinese protectorate, but would have maintained its own government and institutions. This petition was never implemented, and all subsequent Tibetan dialogue initiatives have been rejected by China.

1954

The Dalai Lama travels to Beijing, visits various Chinese cities and addresses the Chinese People's Congress.

He advocates equality, the modernization of society and support to the poor. The Dalai Lama is made vice-president of the Standing Committee of the People's Congress of the People's Republic of China.

India recognizes Tibet as an 'Autonomous Region of China'.

Tenzin Norbu Namseling ('Tenor'), the elder brother of Tendöl, is born in Lhasa. The Dalai Lama recognizes him in 1957 as a reincarnation of the fifth Khado Rinpoche.

1955

The Dalai Lama returns to Tibet from China with the tenth Panchen Lama. He says in a speech that the 'Chinese want to help Tibet' and advocates secular reforms in a Buddhist and autonomous Tibet. Influential Tibetans resist this strategy and distrust China.

1957/ 1958

Choekyi, 28, makes a fictitious 'pilgrimage' to Kalimpong (India) with her daughters Soyang, Dolkar, Tenzing, and Ngodup, as well as her son Tenor and his half-sister Sodon and cousin Pema. Choekyi's three older daughters are enrolled in St. Joseph's Convent in Kalimpong. She herself returns to Lhasa after five months with her two youngest, Ngodup and Tenor.

In mid-October 1958, Jigme Paljor Namseling is sent to Lhokha (southeastern Tibet) by the Tibetan government, under Chinese pressure, to disperse the Tibetan resistance force, Chushi Gangdruk. He delivers the message, but instead of dissolving the group, he joins (to the surprise of the Chinese generals) the uprising of the Khampa. At the time of her husband's departure, Choekyi ist three months pregnant with Tendöl.

1959

10 March: Uprising of the Tibetans. Mao telegraphs to Lhasa: 'The Tibetan problems must be solved by force.' Thousands of Tibetans are killed, the Dalai Lama flees to India on 17 March. Still on Tibetan soil, he revokes the '17-Point Agreement'. As 'supreme spiritual leader' India grants him asylum. The Dalai Lama is allowed to administer a 'Tibetan Central Administration' in Dharamsala, but (officially) not an exile government.

Birth of Tenzin Dolma ('Tendöl') in the midst of the uprising in Lhasa. Father Paljor Jigme finds himself in southern Tibet on the path of the fleeing Dalai Lama. In May he escapes Tibet and arrives at his daughters' home in Kalimpong. He will never meet his youngest daughter, Tendöl, and never again see his wife, Choekyi, who lives in Tibet.

1959, 1961, 1965

The UN General Assembly passes several resolutions condemning human rights violations in Tibet.

1960

Tendöl's sisters, Dolkar and Tenzing, arrive at the Pestalozzi Village in Trogen, Switzerland, where they grow up far from their parents. Twenty years later (1980) Dolkar receives the first letter from her released mother.

1965

The TAR (Tibet Autonomous Region) is officially proclaimed as part of the People's Republic of China.

1966–1976

During the terror and anarchy of the Cultural Revolution, almost all monasteries and religious institutions are destroyed in Tibet, and monks and nuns arrested, disrobed and tortured.

1970

Tendöl turns eleven. Her sixteen-year-old brother Tenor is imprisoned and spends three years in solitary confinement. Her mother, Choekyi, is first detained, then arrested, and spends almost ten years in prison.

1972–1974

Tendöl, thirteen, attends M'ang Tsuk School in Lhasa.

1973

Tendöl's brother Tenor is released but has to stay in Lhasa and work in a quarry.

Her father Paljor Jigme Namseling dies in Gangtok (Sikkim), in the home of his eldest daughter Soyang, married to the youngest son of the Chögyal, the ruler of Sikkim.

1975

Tendöl is sent to labour on road construction in Kongpo, near the Indian border.

1979

Mother Choekyi, acquitted on probation, turns fifty-one and is in poor health. Daughter Soyang and niece Pema visit Choekyi in Lhasa. Last time they met was 1958, when Choekyi took her eldest daughters and Pema to Kalimpong, India.

Deng Xiaoping, general secretary of the Chinese Communist Party, declares that 'Everything but the independence of Tibet can be negotiated.' The Dalai Lama communicates with the Chinese leadership.

His goal: To preserve Tibet's political, cultural and religious autonomy within the People's Republic of China. China repeatedly refuses the Tibetans' calls for dialogue.

1980

Tendöl starts a motor mechanic apprenticeship in Lhasa.

1981

Choekyi, Ngodup and Tendöl are permitted to leave Tibet. They go to Dharamsala via Nepal.
Tenor is retained in Tibet.

1982

Tendöl arrives with her mother in Switzerland. They are reunited at Pestalozzi Children's Village with Dolkar and Tenzing, who have not seen their mother for twenty-four years, and meet Tendöl for the first time.

1985

Tendöl receives political asylum in Switzerland.

1986

Tendöl marries Chungtag, a Tibetan raised in Switzerland. Birth of Tenzin Kelden (1986) and Jigmi (1989).

1989

The Dalai Lama receives the Nobel Peace Prize.

1996

Tendöl opens a shop in the old town of Bern with two partners.

1997

Tendöl's sisters open their 'Little Tibet' shop in Zurich's old town.

2002

Tendöl travels to Lhasa.

2006

Tendöl marries for the second time.

Choekyi travels to Tibet with her niece, Pema, and visits Namseling Manor.

2011

The Dalai Lama retires as political leader of the Tibetans and devolves his political responsibility to the elected political leadership of the exile government. The election takes place every 5 years.

2014

Choekyi dies in Mumbai at the age of eighty-three.

2016

Tendöl opens her own shop 'Lhasa Boutique' in Bern's old
  town.

Acknowledgments

Just before she turned sixty–as did the Tibetan uprising–Tendöls dearest wish was to tell her painful story and to dedicate this little book to all Tibetans who up to this day courageously stand up against China. She opened her heart and recounted the tragic events without the slightest hint of bitterness or hatred, with the mindfulness of a true Buddhist. I admire and thank her for that.

My thanks also go to her family, especially Tenzin Kelden, Tseten and Dolkar, who always assisted me with words and deeds. I thank Pema and Ngodup for their personal reports from the USA, Tsering Woeser for the dramatic images from her archive and Tenor for the photos from his youth. I thank the historian, Wangpo Tethong, for his critical checking of the political events, Christophe

Besuchet for the map he designed, Jane Perkins as well as Afeefa Anjum Baig and Shreya Punj, the editors of Penguin Random House, India, for meticulously editing the English translation. It was a pleasure to discuss the layout with Dhondup Roder and to find suitable places for the unique pictures from Tendöl's childhood.

The royalties of this book are donated to Gu-Chu-Sum, a non-profit organisation on behalf of former political prisoners of Tibet. www.guchusum.in